## The Urbana Free Library

To renew: call 217-367-4057
or go to "*urbanafreelibrary.org*"
and select "Renew/Request Items"

# THE CASE OF
## The Infected Tick

## Michelle Faulk, PhD

**Enslow Publishers, Inc.**
40 Industrial Road
Box 398
Berkeley Heights, NJ 07922
USA

http://www.enslow.com

Library of Congress Cataloging-in-Publication Data

Faulk, Michelle
    The case of the infected tick : Annie Biotica solves circulatory system disease
        crimes / Michelle Faulk.
        p. cm. — (Body system disease investigations)
    Includes index.
    ISBN 978-0-7660-3948-3
    1. Tick-borne diseases—Juvenile literature. 2. Ticks as carriers of disease—
        Juvenile literature. I. Title.
    RA641.T5F38 2013
    571.9'86—dc23                          2011041880

Future editions:
Paperback ISBN 978-1-4644-0226-5
ePUB ISBN 978-1-4645-1139-4
PDF ISBN 978-1-4646-1139-1

Printed in China
062012 Leo Paper Group, Heshan City, Guangdong, China

10 9 8 7 6 5 4 3 2 1

**To Our Readers:** We have done our best to make sure all Internet Addresses in this book were active and appropriate when we went to press. However, the author and the publisher have no control over and assume no liability for the material available on those Internet sites or on other Web sites they may link to. Any comments or suggestions can be sent by e-mail to comments@enslow.com or to the address on the back cover.

**Illustration Credits:** Carol and Mike Werner/Phototake, p. 31; CDC/James Gathany, p. 10 (bottom); Enslow Publishers, Inc., p. 24 (top); Illustrations by Jeff Weigel (www. jeffweigel.com), pp. 1, 3, 5, 9, 13, 15, 19, 21, 25, 27, 31, 33, 37, 38, 40, 42, 46, 47; National Cancer Institute, p. 15; Photo Researchers, Inc.: Biophoto Associates, pp. 23, 24 (bottom), BSIP, p. 36 (bottom), CNRI, p. 27, Dr. P. Marazzi, pp. 29, 34, 37, James Cavallini, p. 28, Juergen Berger, pp. 11 (top), 12, NIBSC, p. 16 (bottom), Scott Camazine, p. 11 (bottom); Pixland/Photos.com, p. 40; Shutterstock.com, pp. 6, 7, 8, 10 (top), 14, 16 (top, middle), 17, 19, 20, 21, 22, 25, 30, 32, 36 (top), 38, 42.

**Cover Illustration:** Illustrations by Jeff Weigel (www.jeffweigel.com)

# Contents

My name is **Agent Annie Biotica**. I am a Disease Scene Investigator with the Major Health Crimes Unit. My job is to keep people safe from the troublemaker germs out there. How do I do it? I use logic and the scientific method. I gather clues from health crime scenes. I identify microbe suspects. I gather evidence. If all goes well I get justice for the victims by curing them. Sometimes all doesn't go well. These are some of my stories.

*Annie Biotica*

# The Human Circulatory System

The circulatory system contains the heart, blood, and blood vessels. It supplies our cells with oxygen and nutrients and removes carbon dioxide.

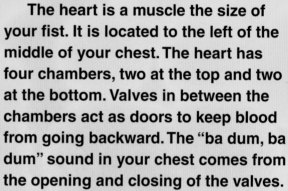

The heart is a muscle the size of your fist. It is located to the left of the middle of your chest. The heart has four chambers, two at the top and two at the bottom. Valves in between the chambers act as doors to keep blood from going backward. The "ba dum, ba dum" sound in your chest comes from the opening and closing of the valves.

The heart has three layers of tissue. The outside layer covers and cushions the heart. The middle layer is thick cardiac muscle. The thin inside layer lines the chambers and valves.

The heart is contained inside a double-walled sac filled with fluid. The sac anchors the heart in place and separates it from other organs. It gives the heart room to expand when beating.

A little more than half of our blood is liquid called plasma. Plasma is yellow and contains hormones,

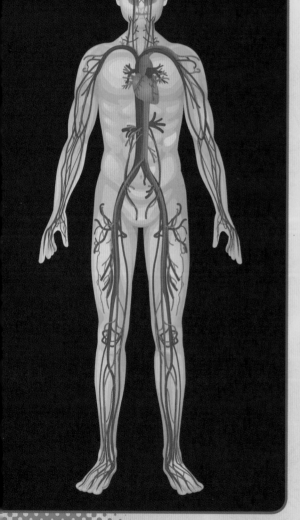

*The heart, blood, and blood vessels make up the circulatory system.*

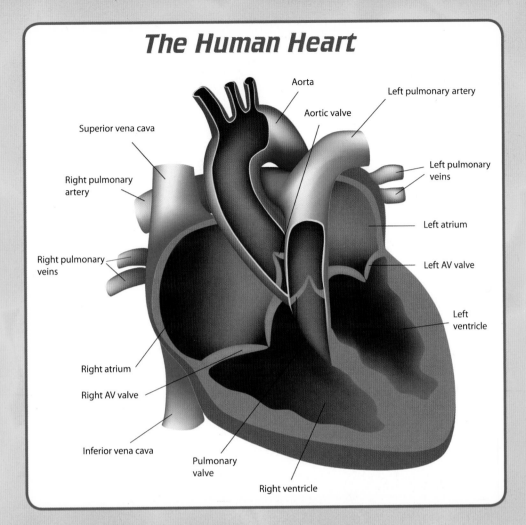

# The Human Heart

Aorta

Aortic valve

Left pulmonary artery

Superior vena cava

Right pulmonary artery

Left pulmonary veins

Left atrium

Right pulmonary veins

Left AV valve

Left ventricle

Right atrium

Right AV valve

Inferior vena cava

Pulmonary valve

Right ventricle

nutrients, and waste products made by the body's cells. Three types of cells float in the plasma. Red blood cells (RBCs) deliver oxygen to the body and pick up carbon dioxide. White blood cells (WBCs) fight infections. Platelets help your blood clot when you are bleeding.

The heart pumps blood through tubes called blood vessels. There are three types: arteries, veins, and capillaries. Arteries are the largest and travel away from the heart. Veins are next in size and travel toward the heart. Capillaries are the smallest and link the arteries and veins.

# Chapter 1

# THE CASE OF
# the Infected Tick

## The Crime

During a summer camping trip in Maine, twenty-five-year-old Eric decided he hated bugs. Especially the tiny ones that stick to your skin. Two months later Eric would hate those bugs even more.

# The Clues

In early September, Eric began feeling dizzy and short of breath. When his doctor listened to Eric's heart it seemed to be skipping a beat. The doctor performed an ECG (electrocardiogram). This test can show if the heart is working properly.

Eric's ECG showed that the electrical signal from the top of his heart was not reaching the bottom of his heart. Because the bottom of Eric's heart was not contracting, the heart was skipping a beat. This is called a heart block.

Why did this young, healthy man suddenly have a heart block? Many microbes can attack the heart. This is why I was called in to investigate.

# The Investigation

Eric had had a complete physical back in April and his heart had been fine. He first experienced dizziness and shortness of breath on September 1. What had changed between April and September?

Eric said he got the flu on July 20. Many microbial attacks share the symptoms of flu. I continued to question Eric and found out about the camping trip in Maine. This was two weeks before he had symptoms. Then Eric told me about those annoying bugs. Now I had a suspect.

I showed Eric a series of mug shots. He positively identified the bugs that kept biting him as deer ticks. These bugs are also called black-legged ticks.

Eric said he had noticed a rash on his back after the camping trip. I showed Eric pictures of different types of rashes. He identified his rash as one called erythema migrans (EM). It looks just like a bull's-eye.

Deer ticks, rash, and now heart problems. I believed that Eric had been attacked by a corkscrew-shaped bacterium named *Borrelia burgdorferi*. *B. burgdorferi* loves to hide in deer ticks. It causes Lyme disease. Lyme-infected ticks can be found in many parts of the United States. However, Maine is a hotbed of Lyme attacks.

SUSPECT #1 – DEER TICKS

*Eric identified these deer ticks, AKA black-legged ticks.*

*The picture shows an EM rash. Eric identified this rash as being the same as the one he had on his back.*

These ticks are very tiny and may go unnoticed by the victim. The tick must be attached 24 to 36 hours for the *B. burgdorferi* to leave the tick and enter the person. Since Eric's rash was on his back it makes sense he didn't know there had been a tick there.

Lyme disease has three stages. Stage 1 is when the bacteria first enter the body and cause the EM rash and then flu-like symptoms. In Stage 2, the bacteria can begin to attack muscles, nerves, joints, and the heart. Months or years later the victim may enter Stage 3, when the bacteria have spread throughout the body.

Based on the infection timeline and Eric's symptoms, I believed the victim was in Stage 2 of Lyme disease.

SUSPECT #2 – BORRELIA BURGDORFERI

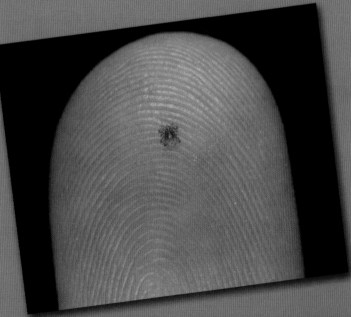

*Deer ticks are very tiny!*

As is usual with Lyme disease attacks, the health crime court accepted Eric's exposure to ticks, his EM rash, and his particular heart problem as evidence of Lyme disease.

## ✔ The Verdict

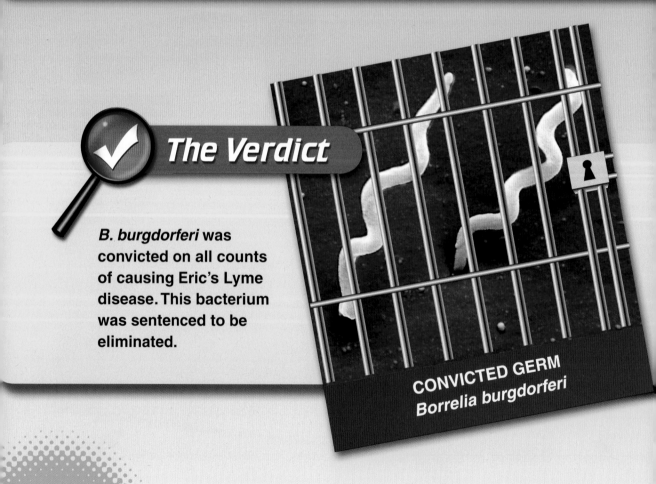

*B. burgdorferi* was convicted on all counts of causing Eric's Lyme disease. This bacterium was sentenced to be eliminated.

**CONVICTED GERM**
*Borrelia burgdorferi*

# *Justice*

Eric was given antibiotics for four weeks to kill any remaining *B. burgdorferi* bacteria in his body. Because Eric's heart had been attacked by this bacteria he was kept in the hospital. Eric was a young man and got treatment early enough, so he was able to fully recover from his attack.

*This is Agent Annie Biotica signing off. Stay safe out there.*

# Chapter 2

# THE CASE OF
## the *Dirty Needle*
## (HIV)

## *The Crime*

When Daniel was twenty years old, he began using drugs. Eight years later Daniel's family convinced him to give up drugs. Daniel went to a drug rehabilitation center for help. When he arrived he wasn't feeling well so he was sent to the hospital. Daniel may have quit drugs, but they were still killing him.

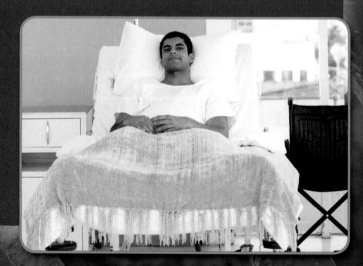

# The Clues

When I met Daniel these were his symptoms:

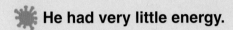 He had very little energy.

He was nearly twenty pounds underweight.

He often had fevers and sweats.

He had several strange purple splotches on his skin.

# The Suspect

The symptom that caught my attention was the purple splotches on Daniel's skin. Most were flat but a few were raised up a little. They did not itch or cause him pain. I took a small piece of one and examined it under the microscope. I recognized the cells. The marks were Kaposi sarcomas.

Kaposi sarcomas are a type of cancer.

*The Kaposi sarcomas on Daniel's skin*

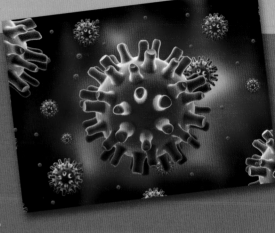

*The human herpes virus 8 caused Daniel's Kaposi sarcomas.*

They are caused by the human herpes virus 8 (HHV-8). A healthy person can fight off HHV-8 attacks. There must have been something wrong with Daniel's immune system if HHV-8 had gotten the best of him.

Many people with Kaposi sarcomas have been attacked by a deadly virus called Human Immunodeficiency Virus (HIV). This virus infects and kills a type of white blood cell called a CD4 cell. These cells are also part of the immune system. As the body loses these important cells it becomes an easy target to any microbial thug that comes along.

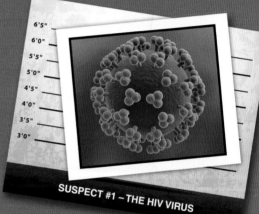

SUSPECT #1 – THE HIV VIRUS

It was very likely that the HIV had entered Daniel when he shared a needle with an HIV-positive person. The virus had hitched a ride in a tiny bit of blood from that person. Daniel had unknowingly injected himself with the virus along with the drugs. Although the HIV can be passed from one person to another through shared needles, it is also a sexually transmitted disease (STD) and is most often contracted by sexual contact.

*A CD4 cell is covered with HIV (red).*

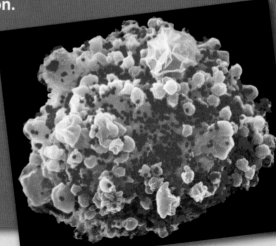

# *The Evidence*

## Test One — The Polymerase Chain Reaction (PCR) Test

I took a sample of Daniel's blood. The PCR test uses small pieces of genetic material (DNA or RNA) called primers. The primers find and stick to the genetic material inside the HIV. An enzyme is added that copies the genetic material inside the HIV. Once the virus's genetic material is copied a million times over, the amount is measured using computerized machines.

*Result:* Daniel's blood contained a lot of HIV. He had 40,000 viruses per milliliter of blood.

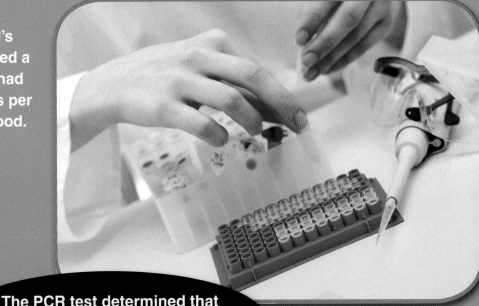

The PCR test determined that Daniel's blood contained a high number of HIV.

## Measure Daniel's CD4 Cells

To perform this test I used a machine called a flow cytometer. This machine takes a sample of the victim's cells and forces them one at a time past a measuring device. A computer is able to recognize what type of cell passes by and keeps count of them.

*Result:* Daniel had only 170 CD4 cells per microliter of blood. Being HIV positive and having less than 200 CD4 cells per microliter of blood meant that Daniel had AIDS. AIDS is the last and worst stage of being infected with HIV.

AIDS stands for:
Acquired – This disease comes from a microbial infection.
Immune – It is the immune system that is attacked in this infection.
Deficiency – The immune system becomes deficient. This means it loses its CD4 cells.
Syndrome – This disease has many symptoms.

The Case of the Infected Tick

# The Verdict

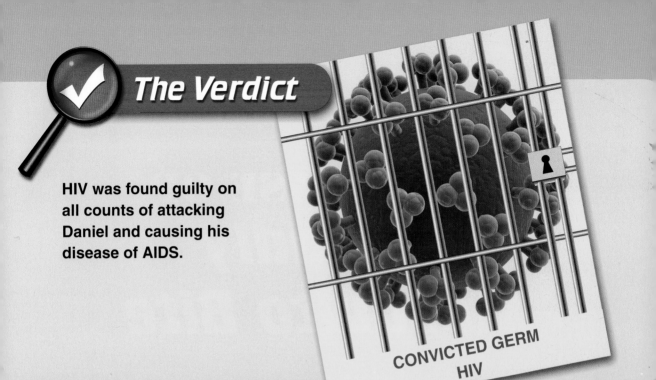

HIV was found guilty on all counts of attacking Daniel and causing his disease of AIDS.

**CONVICTED GERM HIV**

# Justice

Unfortunately there is no cure for HIV. There are only medications that can slow the disease. Daniel was diagnosed late in his illness. Despite taking these medications he died sixteen months after being diagnosed.

*This is Agent Annie Biotica signing off. Stay safe out there.*

# Chapter 3

# THE CASE OF
## the *Deadly*
## *Mosquito Bite*

## The Crime

Velda was turning sixty-five years old. She decided to take a trip with a volunteer group to West Africa where they built a new school. Velda returned from Africa two months later. Unfortunately, she brought home an unexpected souvenir.

# The Clues

Velda got a very bad headache ten days after she got home. She was also tired, nauseated, and vomiting. At the doctor's office, her temperature was 104°F. Velda told the doctor that her symptoms seemed to last a few days and then she would feel all right for a few days. The doctor said that Velda was probably experiencing a viral attack and sent her home.

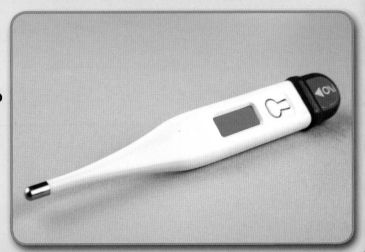

The next day Velda's fever was worse and she was shaking with chills. Velda's daughter took her to the emergency room. That's when I got the call.

# The Suspects

When I interviewed Velda I admired her unique jewelry. She said she had gotten it recently in Africa. I was immediately concerned. Africa is a beautiful continent but it is filled with some microbial outlaws. Velda's "on and off" symptoms made me suspect malaria.

Malaria is the disease caused by protozoa in the crime family of *Plasmodium*. These creatures hide in the saliva of female *Anopheles* mosquitoes. When an infected mosquito bites a person, *Plasmodium* enter the victim's bloodstream. They first travel to the victim's liver before attacking red blood cells (RBCs). As RBCs die the victim begins to experience disease symptoms.

There are four *Plasmodium* gangsters that commit malaria attacks:

 *Plasmodium falciparum*

 *Plasmodium vivax*

 *Plasmodium malariae*

 *Plasmodium ovale*

I needed to identify Velda's trespasser.

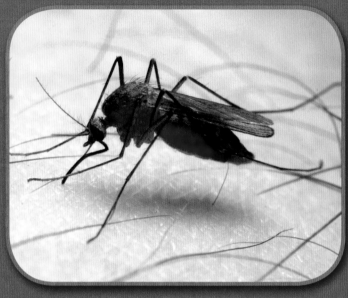

*The* Anopheles *mosquito spreads malaria.*

## Fast Fact!

Depending on which species of *Plasmodium* has attacked, the disease can be mild or deadly. *P. falciparum* and *P. vivax* are the most common infections. *P. falciparum* is the most deadly.

# The Evidence

## Are *Plasmodia* in Velda's Bloodstream?

I took a small amount of Velda's blood, smeared it on a microscope slide, and performed a Giemsa stain. This is a special stain for blood cells that will let me see if parasites are hiding inside them. (The parasites stain dark blue inside the lighter blue red blood cells in the photo below.)

*Result:* I saw *Plamsmodia* inside Velda's red blood cells. Using mug shots, I identified her attacker as *P. falciparum*.

*P. falciparum* is deadly. To end its streak of terror I needed a second positive ID.

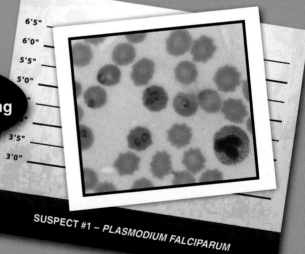

SUSPECT #1 – PLASMODIUM FALCIPARUM

The Giemsa stain revealed the darker *P. falciparum* hiding inside Velda's blood cells.

# Rapid Diagnostic Test for *Plasmodium falciparum*

These tests are kits made by various companies for diagnosing malaria. They take less than one hour.

I mixed a sample of Velda's blood with a chemical that burst her RBCs. This releases *Plasmodium*. Anti-*P. falciparum* antibodies were added. The end of a strip of special paper was held in the blood mixture. As the liquid traveled up the paper strip it met a line of different antibodies. If these grabbed onto *P. falciparum* a color reaction would create a visible line on the paper.

*Result:* There was a colored line on the paper strip. This meant that *P. falciparum* was the protozoa inside Velda's RBCs.

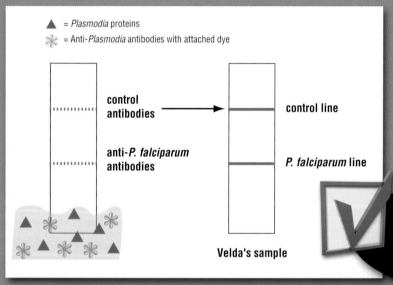

▲ = *Plasmodia* proteins

✳ = Anti-*Plasmodia* antibodies with attached dye

control antibodies → control line

anti-*P. falciparum* antibodies — *P. falciparum* line

Velda's sample

The rapid diagnostic test for *Plasmodium falciparum* confirmed that Velda had been attacked by this microbe.

# The Verdict

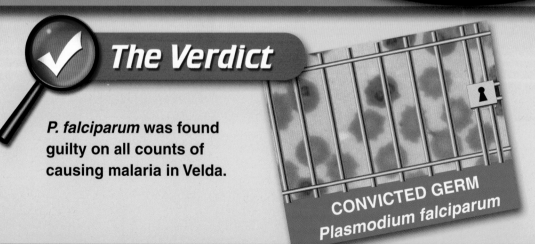

*P. falciparum* was found guilty on all counts of causing malaria in Velda.

CONVICTED GERM
*Plasmodium falciparum*

# Justice

Velda had been attacked by the worst of the malaria offenders.

🦠 Many of her RBCs had been destroyed.

🦠 The dead RBCs had clogged Velda's blood vessels, preventing her brain from getting oxygen.

🦠 Her urine had turned almost black because the dying RBCs were releasing a protein called hemoglobin. This condition is called blackwater-fever.

Velda remained in the hospital and received a strong anti-malaria drug. She also received a blood transfusion to replace her blood and get oxygen to her brain. Four days later I repeated the Giemsa stain and saw no *P. falciparum*. In time, Velda made a full recovery.

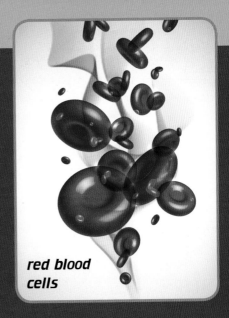
red blood cells

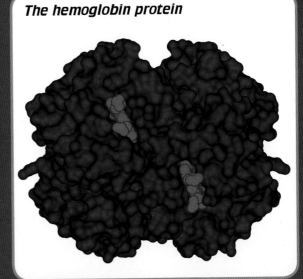
The hemoglobin protein

*This is Agent Annie Biotica signing off. Stay safe out there.*

# Chapter 4

# THE CASE OF
## the *Broken Heart*

## The Crime

Seventy-two-year-old Todd went to the hospital to visit his son who had been in a car accident. As he entered the building, he suddenly felt very sick. He made it up to his son's room and sank into a chair. When the doctor came into the room he saw Todd leaning over in his chair, pale and sweating. The doctor was immediately concerned and moved Todd to an examination room. The doctor was right to be concerned, because Todd was dying.

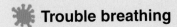

These were Todd's symptoms:

- Trouble breathing
- Fatigue
- Heart pounding in his chest

The doctor listened to Todd's heart. He heard a low-pitched rumbling sound. The doctor knew that this sound indicated mitral valve stenosis (MVS). This occurs when the valve on the left side of the heart becomes thick and stiff with scar tissue. The scar tissue prevents the valve from opening correctly. Blood flow is reduced. The doctor also knew that MVS is often the result of a microbial health crime. That was when I was called in.

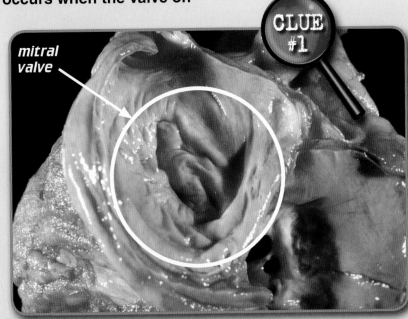

*This is an example of what mitral valve stenosis looks like. The mitral valve is not supposed to be this thick and narrow.*

# The Suspect

To confirm that Todd had MVS I performed a sonogram. A machine sends sound waves into the body. As the waves bounce back to a computer, an image of the heart is produced. I immediately saw that Todd's heart valve was not opening as far as it should. Todd definitely had MVS.

Many people Todd's age with MVS have survived a microbial attack that occurred a long time ago. The attack I suspected was rheumatic fever. The culprit is the bacterium *Streptococcus pyogenes*. This is the bacterium that causes strep throat. Antibiotics are very effective at curing strep throat. However, before 1943 antibiotics were not available. Strep throat attacks lasted longer, sometimes long enough for *S. pyogenes* to cause the second disease, rheumatic fever.

*This is a sonogram of a healthy heart. The numbered dark spaces show the four chambers of the heart. Each is surrounded by the heart walls (dark red and blue areas). A healthy mitral valve separates chambers 2 and 4. Todd's sonogram did not look like this.*

The *S. pyogenes* bacterium causes rheumatic fever by confusing the body's immune system. *S. pyogenes* has proteins that look very similar to proteins found in the human heart. Some people's immune systems are tricked into attacking the heart along with the bacteria. Before antibiotics were available, many rheumatic fever victims died. Health crime investigators have discovered that many of the survivors suffered permanent heart damage that went unnoticed for many years.

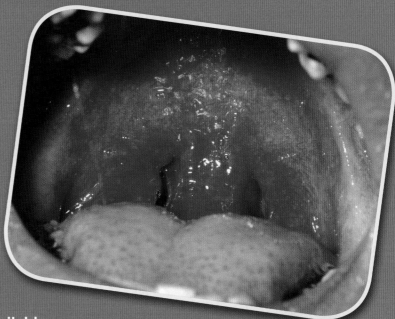

*The bacterium* Streptococcus pyogenes *causes strep throat.*

## The Evidence

Todd confirmed that he had rheumatic fever when he was ten years old. The evidence linking *S. pyogenes* to Todd's MVS is the long history of people who survived rheumatic fever and then experienced mitral valve disease later in life.

## The Verdict

Todd's previous rheumatic fever attack and his current heart disease were enough to convince the health crimes court that *S. pyogenes* was guilty of causing Todd's heart damage.

**CONVICTED GERM**
*Streptococcus pyogenes*

The *S. pyogenes* that caused Todd's heart disease were long gone. Antibiotics were no good now. It was his heart that needed fixing. Todd was taken into surgery where a balloon valvotomy was performed. A very thin and flexible tube was inserted into an artery in Todd's arm. Eventually the tube reached his heart. On the tip of this tube was a small balloon. When the balloon was inside the opening of the damaged valve it was inflated. This stretched the valve tissue so it would work better.

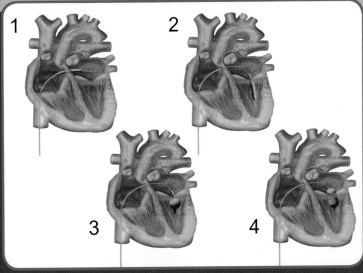

*During Todd's mitral balloon valvotomy, a thin flexible tube was threaded into the heart (1) until the balloon tip was in the mitral valve (2). The balloon was slowly inflated (3) until the mitral valve was fully stretched open (4).*

Todd immediately felt better and went home in a few days. A balloon valvotomy is not a cure for mitral valve stenosis. It only reduces the symptoms. Todd will have to routinely see a heart doctor to keep an eye on that valve. At some point he may even need to have the valve replaced with a man-made one.

*This is Agent Annie Biotica signing off. Stay safe out there.*

# Chapter 5

# THE CASE OF
## the *Microbial Bully*

## The Crime

Luzia was fifteen years old when her parents moved to a new state. She had a lot of trouble adjusting to her new school. A group of girls had decided to bully her. Luzia became so miserable that she often fibbed to her mother that she was sick. This allowed her to avoid school for a day or two.

*Because Luzia was being bullied at her new school she tried to stay home a lot.*

Eventually, the bullies stopped bothering Luzia, and Luzia felt a lot better. She began to make new friends and started to enjoy her new school. One day Luzia really did feel sick and told her mother. Because she had fibbed so many times before, her mother didn't believe her. Luzia was sent off to school. Later that day the school nurse called her mother. Luzia needed to see a doctor. It seemed that Luzia was being bullied by a microbe this time.

# The Clues

The doctor noted that Luzia had a mild fever, a sore throat, and was very tired. The doctor decided this was a minor health crime. He gave Luzia medicine for her fever and sent her home.

Luzia took all the medicine but a week later she still felt very ill. Luzia's mother decided she needed to go to the emergency room. That's when I got the call.

When I met Luzia at the hospital these were her symptoms:

- A very red and sore throat

- Swollen lymph nodes on her neck

- A low fever

- A swollen spleen and liver

Luzia's previous doctor had made a quick diagnosis of a common sore throat. But the symptoms Luzia was experiencing often indicate an attack by the Epstein-Barr (EB) virus.

*The Epstein-Barr virus causes infectious mononucleosis.*

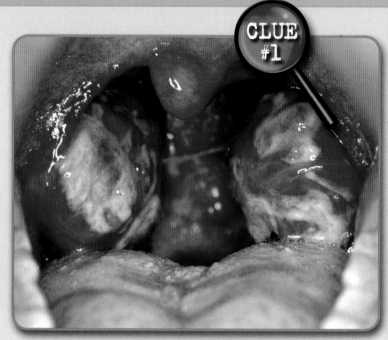

*Luzia's sore throat*

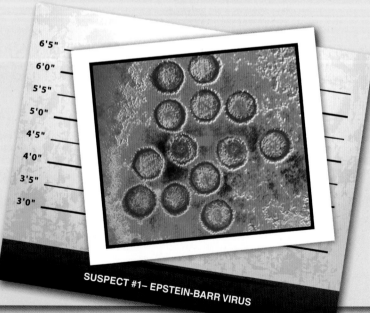

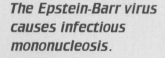

SUSPECT #1– EPSTEIN-BARR VIRUS

# The Suspect

The EB virus is a microbial lawbreaker that seems to be everywhere. Over 90 percent of adults in the United States have been victims. This virus causes a disease called infectious mononucleosis (mono). The EB virus enters the nose or mouth and invades the B cells of the immune system. Once inside the B cells, more EB viruses are produced. The infected B cells travel throughout the body and spread the virus to the liver and spleen. This is why Luzia's liver and spleen were swollen. This is also why her neck lymph nodes were swollen.

There was a lot of visible evidence suggesting that the EB virus had attacked Luzia. However, I wanted laboratory evidence to close the case.

# The Evidence

 **A Monospot Test**

A monospot test detects the anti-EB antibodies that are made when someone is attacked by the EB virus. These antibodies are special because they also stick to the red blood cells (RBC) of a horse.

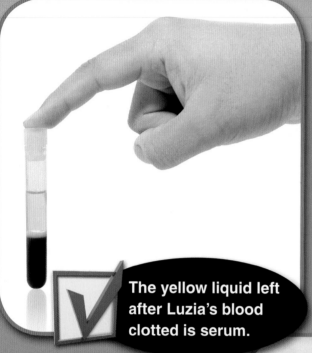

I took a sample of Luzia's blood. I let the blood clot in the test tube. The liquid on top is called serum. A drop of Luzia's serum was placed on a microscope slide. The chemicals from a monospot test that I bought from a company were added. After ten minutes I examined the slide under the microscope.

The yellow liquid left after Luzia's blood clotted is serum.

*Result:* Luzia's serum had made the sample clump together. This meant that her body had made anti-EB antibodies.

The result was positive for EB virus because Luzia's RBCs clumped together during the monospot test.

The Case of the Infected Tick

# The Verdict

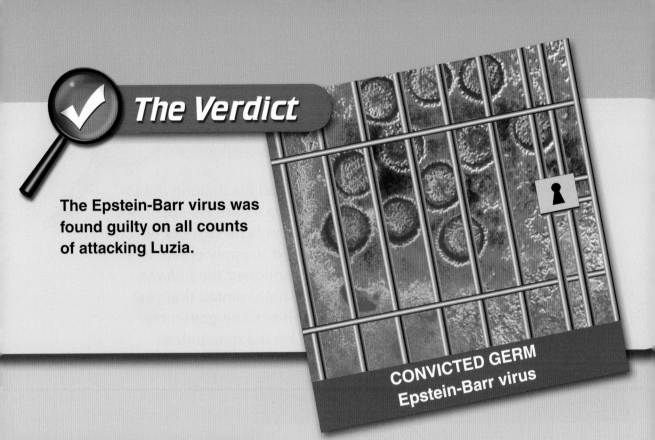

The Epstein-Barr virus was found guilty on all counts of attacking Luzia.

**CONVICTED GERM**
Epstein-Barr virus

# Justice

There is no cure for EB virus. It was up to Luzia's immune system to fight this war. The fight took three months, but Luzia's body was victorious.

*This is Agent Annie Biotica signing off. Stay safe out there.*

# You Solve the Case

A forty-seven-year-old man named Tom had his lifelong dream come true. He won a trip to Africa to go on safari! He spent two weeks in Africa. He loved all the wild animals he saw but he hated the mosquitoes. Every night he had to apply cream to all the bites he had gotten that day. Tom mentioned the bites to his safari guide. His guide said that the high rainfall that year caused the mosquitoes to be a real problem. The government was even spraying pesticides to try to kill the mosquitoes.

Two weeks after returning home Tom felt very sick. His son drove him to the emergency room. These were his symptoms:

🦠 Headache

🦠 Nausea and vomiting

🦠 Extreme fatigue

🦠 Fever

🦠 Sweating and chills

The doctor thought he knew what was ailing Tom, so he asked him this question: Did his symptoms last for a few days and then go away for a few days? The patient answered yes.

1. What disease would you suspect?

2. What microbial culprit would you suspect?

3. What type of microbe is the culprit?

4. Is an insect an accomplice in this health crime?

# You Solve the Case

William and a group of his college friends went on a weekend camping trip in Massachusetts. The weather was sunny and hot—so hot that every day and night the group wore short-sleeved T-shirts and shorts. William and his friends did a lot of hiking and enjoyed sleeping outside in tents. Besides some sunburn, the bugs were a real nuisance. There were these very tiny ones that really stuck to their skin. One of the girls had brought a pair of tweezers. The friends laughed at how they

The Case of the Infected Tick

took turns pulling these crazy bugs off each other. The weird thing was that William and several of his friends came home with a strange rash. Then two weeks later everyone with the rash came down with what seemed like the flu. These were the symptoms:

- Feeling tired

- Headache

- Fever and chills

- Muscle and joint pain

At the college's medical center William and his friends were diagnosed. They were treated with antibiotics and eventually recovered.

1. What disease would you suspect?

2. What microbe causes this disease?

3. Is an insect involved in this health crime?

# You Solve the Case

CASE #3

The year is 1930. A fifteen-year-old girl named Patricia lies in bed very ill. These are her symptoms:

- A red and swollen throat that is extremely painful

- Small white spots on the tissue of her throat

- Breath that smells like rotten food

- A fever of 104°F

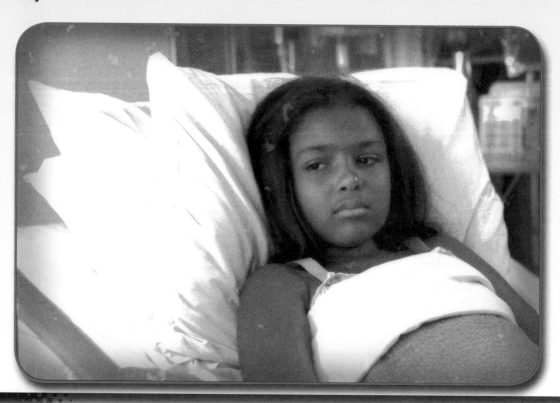

After Patricia had been lying in bed sick for several weeks, her family became very worried. She seemed to be getting worse. She had lost a lot of weight, was very pale, and had a strange rash on her body. Even though the family was very poor, they sent for a doctor. The doctor examined Patricia and told her parents that she had rheumatic fever. Patricia's mother started crying because one of Patricia's playmates down the street had just died of the same disease. The doctor said he was sorry, but there was little he could do for Patricia. Luckily, Patricia did not die from this health crime.

1. What microbe causes rheumatic fever?

2. Why did the doctor not prescribe antibiotics for Patricia?

3. Patricia survived her rheumatic fever attack, but what health problems may she have in the future?

# You Solve the Case: The Answers

## CASE #1 — Malaria

**What disease would you suspect?** The symptoms, the trip to Africa, and the mosquito bites all point to malaria.

**What microbial culprit would you suspect?** One of the members of the *Plasmodium* crime family.

**What type of microbe is the culprit?** A protozoan.

**Is an insect an accomplice in this health crime?** Yes. *Plasmodium* hides in the saliva of the *Anopheles* mosquitoes.

## CASE #2 — Lyme Disease

**What disease would you suspect?** Lyme disease.

**What microbe causes this disease?** A corkscrew shaped bacterium called *Borrelia burgdorferi.*

**Is an insect involved in this health crime?** Yes. This *B. burgdorferi* is spread to people and pets by the deer tick. It is also called a black-legged tick.

## CASE #3 — Rheumatic Fever

**What microbe causes rheumatic fever?** The bacterium *Streptococcus pyogenes.* Rheumatic fever usually follows an attack of strep throat, a crime committed by the same bacteria.

**Why did the doctor not prescribe antibiotics for Patricia?** Antibiotics were not yet available to the public.

**What health problems may Patricia have in the future?** During rheumatic fever the heart valves may become damaged. Later in life Patricia may have mitral valve stenosis.

# Glossary

**antibiotics:** Medicines that inhibit the growth of bacteria.

**antibodies:** Proteins made by the body that help fight off invaders.

**B cell:** A cell made by the immune system. It can recognize invading microbes and begin to make antibodies.

**capillaries:** Extremely small blood vessels. They connect the arteries and veins.

**CD4 cell:** A type of cell that is made by the immune system. It is also called a T-helper cell.

**DNA:** A stringy material inside cells that contains genes. It contains the sugar deoxyribose.

**enzyme:** A protein that performs a chemical reaction.

**erythema migrans:** A specific type of rash observed in Lyme disease. It looks like a bull's-eye.

**extracellular fluid:** The fluid that surrounds cells of the body.

**infection:** Disease that occurs when live microbes enter the body.

**lymph nodes:** Oval-shaped masses of tissue. They filter lymph fluid. There are 500-600 in the body.

**plasma:** The liquid part of blood. Blood is made up of plasma and cells.

**platelets:** Small cell fragments that help the blood to clot. They do not have a nucleus.

# Glossary

**primers:** Small pieces of DNA that find and stick to the DNA inside a microbe.

**RNA:** A type of genetic material that contains the sugar ribose.

**serum:** The liquid that is left when blood is allowed to clot.

Dicker, Katie. *AIDS and HIV.* New York: Rosen Central, 2011.

Hoffmann, Gretchen. *Mononucleosis.* Tarrytown, N.Y.: Marshall Cavendish, 2006.

Lynette, Rachel. *Malaria.* Farmington Hills, Mich.: KidHaven Press, 2006.

Whittemore, Susan. *The Circulatory System.* New York: Chelsea House, 2009.

Yannielli, Len. *Lyme Disease.* New York: Chelsea House, 2004.

## Internet Addresses

American Lyme Disease Foundation
<http://www.aldf.com>

Centers for Disease Control and Prevention (CDC). "Malaria."
<http://www.cdc.gov/malaria/index.html>

# Index

## A
Acquired Immune Deficiency Syndrome (AIDS), 18, 19
*Anopheles* mosquito, 22, 44
antibiotics, 13, 28, 29, 31, 41, 43, 44
antibodies, 24, 35, 36
arteries, 7

## B
B cells, 35
balloon valvotomy, 31
black-legged ticks. *See* deer ticks
blackwater-fever, 25
blood, 6, 7, 16, 17, 18, 22, 23, 24, 25, 27, 35, 36
blood vessels, 6, 7, 25
*Borelia burgdorferi* (*B. burgdorferi*), 10–11, 12, 44

## C
capillaries, 7
CD4 cells, 16, 18
circulatory system, 6

## D
deer ticks, 10, 44
DNA, 17

## E
electrocardiogram (ECG), 9
enzyme, 17

## Epstein-Barr (EB) virus, 34, 35, 36, 37
erythema migrans (EM), 10, 11

## G
Glemsa stain, 23, 25

## H
heart, 6
heart block, 9
hemoglobin, 25
human herpes virus 8 (HHV-8), 16
Human Immuno-deficiency Virus (HIV), 16, 17, 19

## K
Kaposi sarcoma, 15, 16

## L
liver, 34, 35
Lyme disease, 10–11, 44
lymph nodes, 34, 35

## M
malaria, 21–22, 24, 44
mitral valve stenosis (MVS), 27, 28, 30, 44
mononucleosis (mono), 35
monospot test, 35

## P
plasma, 6
*Plasmodium*, 22, 23, 44
*P. falciparum*, 23, 24, 25

## platelets, 7
polymerase chain reaction test (PCR test), 17
protozoan, 22, 24, 44

## R
rapid diagnostic test, 24
red blood cells (RBCs), 7, 22, 24, 25, 35, 36
rheumatic fever, 28, 29, 30, 43, 44
RNA, 17

## S
scientific method, 4
serum, 36
sexually transmitted disease (STD), 16
sonogram, 28
spleen, 34, 35
strep throat, 28, 44
*Streptococcus pyogenes* (*S. pyogenes*), 28–29, 30, 31, 44

## V
veins, 7

## W
white blood cells (WBCs), 7, 16